D0092908

KEEP
CALM

YOU'RE ONLY

70

KEEP CALM YOU'RE ONLY 70

Copyright © Summersdale Publishers Ltd, 2011

With text contributed by Vicky Edwards

Summersdale Publishers Ltd
46 West Street
Chichester
West Sussex
PO19 1RP
UK

www.summersdale.com

Printed and bound in the Czech Republic

ISBN: 978-1-84953-228-0

Substantial discounts on bulk quantities of Summersdale books are available to corporations, professional associations and other organisations. For details contact Summersdale Publishers by telephone: +44 (0) 1243 771107, fax: +44 (0) 1243 786300 or email: nicky@summersdale.com.

KEEP
CALM

YOU'RE ONLY

70

summersdale

CONTENTS

ANOTHER
YEAR
OLDER

Being 70 is no different
from being 69. It's a round
number, and there's
something about roundness
that has always appealed.

Elizabeth Taylor

To be 70 years young
is sometimes far more
cheerful and hopeful
than to be 40 years old.

Oliver Wendell Holmes Jr

A diplomat is a man who
always remembers a
woman's birthday but never
remembers her age.

Robert Frost

Our wrinkles are our medals
of the passage of life. They
are what we have been
through and who we
want to be.

Lauren Hutton

My wife hasn't had a
birthday in four years.
She was born in
the year of
Lord-only-knows.

Anonymous

Birthdays are good for you.
Statistics show that the
people who have the most
live the longest.

Larry Lorenzoni

A birthday is just the first day of another 365-day journey around the sun. Enjoy the trip.

Anonymous

For all the advances in
medicine, there is still no cure
for the common birthday.

John Glenn

Our birthdays are
feathers in the broad
wing of time.

Jean Paul Richter

Eventually you will reach a point when you stop lying about your age and start bragging about it.

Will Rogers

Whatever with the past has gone, the best is always yet to come.

Lucy Larcom

If we could be twice young and twice old we could correct all our mistakes.

Euripides

You know you are getting old when the candles cost more than the cake.

Bob Hope

I'm happy to report that my inner child is still ageless.

James Broughton

To be 70 years old is like climbing the Alps. You reach a snow-crowned summit, and see behind you the deep valley stretching miles...

Henry Wadsworth Longfellow

JUST
WHAT
I
ALWAYS
WANTED

A hug is the perfect gift;
one size fits all, and nobody
minds if you exchange it.

Anonymous

Let us celebrate the
occasion with wine and
sweet words.

Plautus

Youth is the gift of nature, but age is a work of art.

Garson Kanin

Yesterday is history,
tomorrow is a mystery,
but today is a gift.
That is why it is called
the present.

Eleanor Roosevelt

When I was young I thought
that money was the most
important thing in life; now
that I am old I know
that it is.

Oscar Wilde

A friend never defends a
husband who gets his wife
an electric skillet for
her birthday.

Erma Bombeck

A gift consists not in
what is done or given,
but in the intention of
the giver or doer.

Seneca

Why is a birthday cake
the only food you can blow
on and spit on and
everybody rushes to
get a piece?

Bobby Kelton

We know we're getting old when the only thing we want for our birthday is not to be reminded of it.

Anonymous

A comfortable old
age is the reward of a
well-spent youth.

Maurice Chevalier

At my age the best gift one can hope for is a continuing sense of humour. The ability to laugh, especially at ourselves, keeps the heart light and the mind young.

Anonymous

There are 364 days when
you might get un-birthday
presents... and only one for
birthday presents, you know.

Lewis Carroll,
Through the Looking Glass

Last week the candle factory burned down. Everyone just stood around and sang 'Happy Birthday'.

Steven Wright

GRIN
AND
BEAR
IT

I will never give in to old age until I become old. And I'm not old yet!

Tina Turner

I still have a full deck; I just shuffle slower now.

Anonymous

I hope I never get so
old I get religious.

Ingmar Bergman

Father Time is not always a hard parent.

Charles Dickens

One of the advantages of
being 70 is that you only
need four hours' sleep. True,
you need it four times
a day, but still.

Denis Norden

Age is a matter of
feeling, not of years.

George William Curtis

I am getting to an age when
I can only enjoy the last
sport left. It is called hunting
for your spectacles.

Edward Grey

Old age is an excellent time for outrage. My goal is to say or do at least one outrageous thing every week.

Maggie Kuhn

You really haven't
changed in 70 years.
Your body changes...
you don't change
at all.

Doris Lessing

The years between 50 and 70 are the hardest. You are always being asked to do more, and you are not yet decrepit enough to turn them down.

T. S. Eliot

Youth disserves;
middle age conserves;
old age preserves.

Martin H. Fischer

Perhaps one has to be very
old before one learns to
be amused rather
than shocked.

Pearl S. Buck

How beautifully leaves
grow old. How full of
light and colour are
their last days.

John Burroughs

I'm growing old; I delight in the past.

Henri Matisse

The longer I live the more
beautiful life becomes.

Frank Lloyd Wright

A healthy old fellow, who is
not a fool, is the happiest
creature living.

Richard Steele

DO
A LITTLE
DANCE
MAKE
A LITTLE
LOVE

I can still enjoy sex at 74. I live at 75, so it's no distance.

Bob Monkhouse

One of the best parts of
growing older? You can flirt
all you like since you've
become harmless.

Liz Smith

How people keep correcting
us when we are young!
There is always some bad
habit or other they tell us we
ought to get over. Yet most
bad habits are tools to help
us through life.

Friedrich Nietzsche

Laughter doesn't
require teeth.

Bill Newton

The more you praise and celebrate your life, the more there is in life to celebrate.

Oprah Winfrey

It's important to
have a twinkle in
your wrinkle.

Anonymous

With mirth and laughter let old wrinkles come.

William Shakespeare

I'd hate to die with a good liver, good kidneys and a good brain. When I die I want everything to be knackered.

Hamish Imlach

I always make a point of
starting the day at 6 a.m.
with champagne. It goes
straight to the heart and
cheers one up.

John Mortimer

If you give up
smoking, drinking
and loving, you don't
actually live longer, it
just seems longer.

Clement Freud

The ageing process has
you firmly in its grasp if you
never get the urge to throw
a snowball.

Doug Larson

You are never too old
to set another goal
or to dream a
new dream.

Les Brown

If you don't learn to laugh
at trouble, you won't have
anything to laugh at
when you're old.

Edgar Watson Howe

Give me chastity and
continence, but
not yet.

Saint Aurelius Augustine

YOUNG
AT
HEART

Old age is always 15 years older than I am.

Oliver Wendell Holmes Sr

I'm saving that rocker for the
day when I feel as old as
I really am.

Dwight D. Eisenhower

Grandmas are mums
with lots of frosting.

Anonymous

Age is just a number. It's totally irrelevant unless, of course, you happen to be a bottle of wine.

Joan Collins

Most grandmas
have a touch of
the scallywag.

Helen Thomson

A woman has the
right to treat the
subject of her age
with ambiguity.

Helena Rubinstein

There are people whose watch stops at a certain hour and who remain permanently at that age.

Charles Augustin Sainte-Beuve

In the midst of winter,
I finally learned that
there was in me an
invincible summer.

Albert Camus

Inside every older person
is a younger person –
wondering what the
hell happened.

Cora Harvey Armstrong

Getting old ain't for sissies.

Bette Davis

I don't want to retire.
I'm not that good at
crossword puzzles.

Norman Mailer

I have a warm feeling
after playing with my
grandchildren. It's the
liniment working.

Anonymous

The secret to staying
young is to live
honestly, eat slowly,
and lie about
your age.

Lucille Ball

I'm not interested in age.
People who tell me their age
are silly. You're as old
as you feel.

Elizabeth Arden

Old age is like everything else. To make a success of it, you've got to start young.

Fred Astaire

Every time I think that I'm getting old, and gradually going to the grave, something else happens.

Elvis Presley

Nature does not equally
distribute energy. Some
people are born old and
tired while others are
going strong at 70.

Dorothy Thompson

When I was a boy the Dead
Sea was only sick.

George Burns

OLDER
AND
WISER?

When they tell me
I'm too old to do
something, I attempt
it immediately.

Pablo Picasso

The more sand has escaped
from the hourglass of our
life, the clearer we should
see through it.

Niccolò Machiavelli

To keep the heart
unwrinkled, to be
hopeful, kindly,
cheerful, reverent –
that is to triumph
over old age.

Thomas Bailey Aldrich

To know how to grow old is
the master work of wisdom,
and one of the most difficult
chapters in the great
art of living.

Henri-Frédéric Amiel

Experience is a
terrible teacher who
sends horrific bills.

Anonymous

I never dared be radical
when young for fear it would
make me conservative
when old.

Robert Frost

We are not limited by
our old age; we are
liberated by it.

Stu Mittleman

Old age is ready to undertake tasks that youth shirked because they would take too long.

W. Somerset Maugham

Age is an opportunity no less than youth itself.

Henry Wadsworth Longfellow

The elderly don't drive that badly; they're just the only ones with time to do the speed limit.

Jason Love

They told me if I got
older I'd get wiser. In
that case I must be
a genius.

George Burns

I've reached an age when
I can't use my youth as an
excuse for my ignorance
any more.

Helen-Janet Bonellie

Few people know how to be old.

François de la Rochefoucauld

Don't just count your years,
make your years count.

Ernest Myers

A man is not old until his
regrets take the place
of dreams.

John Barrymore

No man is ever
old enough to
know better.

Holbrook Jackson

If nothing is going well, call your grandmother.

Italian proverb

There's no fool like an old fool… you can't beat experience.

Jacob Morton Braude

LIVE
LOVE
AND
LAST

I'm too old to do
things by half.

Lou Reed

Few things are more
delightful than grandchildren
fighting over your lap.

Doug Larson

The golden age is before us, not behind us.

William Shakespeare

My grandkids believe I'm
the oldest thing in the world.
And after two or three hours
with them, I believe it, too.

Gene Perret

I want to die in
my sleep like my
grandfather – not
screaming and yelling
like the passengers
in his car.

Wil Shriner

A man is not old
as long as he is
seeking something.

Jean Rostand

At 70, I would say the advantage is that you take life more calmly. You know that 'this, too, shall pass!'

Eleanor Roosevelt

I know one should never say never, but I hope I'll get off the beach before the tide goes out.

Terry Wogan on retirement

You are only young
once, but you can
be immature for
a lifetime.

John P. Grier

And in the end it's not the
years in your life that count.
It's the life in your years.

Abraham Lincoln

Old men should have
more care to end life
well than to live long.

Anita Brookner

Here, with whitened hair, he drank to Life, to all it had been, to what it would be.

Sean O'Casey

Old age, believe me, is a
good and pleasant thing.
It is true you are gently
shouldered off the stage, but
then you are given such a
comfortable front stall
as spectator.

Confucius

If you associate enough
with older people who enjoy
their lives, you will gain the
possibility for a full life.

Margaret Mead

People are always
asking about the good
old days. I say, why
don't you say the
good now days?

Robert M. Young

No cowboy was ever
faster on the draw than a
grandparent pulling a baby
picture out of a wallet.

Anonymous

If I had my life to live over again, I would make the same mistakes, only sooner.

Tallulah Bankhead

No matter what happens,
I'm loud, noisy, earthy and
ready for much more living.

Elizabeth Taylor

ILLS
PILLS
AND
TWINGES

Like everyone else who makes the mistake of getting older, I begin each day with coffee and obituaries.

Bill Cosby

I don't do alcohol any
more – I get the same
effect just standing
up fast.

Anonymous

Beware of the young
doctor and the
old barber.

Benjamin Franklin

When you get to my age life
seems little more than one
long trip to and from
the lavatory.

John Mortimer

Advanced old age is when
you sit in a rocking chair
and can't get it going.

Eliakim Katz

I don't generally feel
anything until noon,
then it's time for
my nap.

Bob Hope

I'm at an age when my back goes out more than I do.

Phyllis Diller

I wish I had the energy that my grandchildren have – if only for self-defence.

Gene Perret

Never worry about
your heart till it
stops beating.

E. B. White

At my age getting a second doctor's opinion is kinda like switching slot machines.

Jimmy Carter

Regular naps prevent
old age, especially
if you take them
while driving.

Anonymous

The trouble with always
trying to preserve the
health of the body is that it
is so difficult to do without
destroying the health
of the mind.

G. K. Chesterton

There's lots of people in this world who spend so much time watching their health that they haven't the time to enjoy it.

Josh Billings

Life expectancy
would grow by leaps
and bounds if green
vegetables smelled as
good as bacon.

Doug Larson

After these two, Dr Diet and
Dr Quiet, Dr Merriman is
requisite to preserve health.

James Howell

CHIN
UP
CHEST
OUT

Every wrinkle but a notch in the quiet calendar of a well-spent life.

Charles Dickens

A married daughter with children puts you in danger of being catalogued as a first edition.

Anonymous

A woman's always younger than a man at equal years.

Elizabeth Barrett Browning

As long as a woman can look ten years younger than her own daughter, she is perfectly satisfied.

Oscar Wilde

Age should not have its face
lifted, but it should rather
teach the world to admire
wrinkles as the etchings
of experience.

Ralph B. Perry

Good cheekbones are
the brassiere of
old age.

Barbara de Portago

Passing the vodka bottle and playing the guitar.

Keith Richards on how he keeps fit

You can't stop the ageing
process. There's only so
much oil you can put
on your body.

Angie Dickinson

How pleasant is the
day when we give up
striving to be young
or slender.

William James

Whenever a man's friends
begin to compliment him
about looking young, he
may be sure that they think
he is growing old.

Washington Irving

I don't plan to grow old
gracefully; I plan to
have facelifts until
my ears meet.

Rita Rudner

Middle age is when
a narrow waist and a
broad mind begin to
change places.

E. Joseph Cossman

Don't retouch my wrinkles…
I would not want it to be
thought that I had lived
for all these years without
something to show for it.

The Queen Mother

Time may be a
great healer, but it's a
lousy beautician.

Anonymous

I'm so wrinkled I can screw my hat on.

Phyllis Diller

I'm like old wine. They
don't bring me out
very often, but I'm
well preserved.

Rose Fitzgerald Kennedy

KEEP
CALM
AND
DRINK
UP

KEEP CALM AND DRINK UP

£4.99

ISBN: 978 1 84953 102 3

'In victory, you deserve champagne; in defeat, you need it.'

Napoleon Bonaparte

BAD ADVICE FOR GOOD PEOPLE.

Keep Calm and Carry On, a World War Two government poster, struck a chord in recent difficult times when a stiff upper lip and optimistic energy were needed again. But in the long run it's a stiff drink and flowing spirits that keep us all going.

Here's a book packed with proverbs and quotations showing the wisdom to be found at the bottom of the glass.

www.summersdale.com